CW00971611

Slow Cooker Recipes

Dolores Kostelni

PORTLAND, OREGON

Cover and Book Design: Kevin A. Welsch, Collectors Press, Inc.
Editors: Lindsay Brown, Collectors Press, Inc., Carole Berglie

Library of Congress Cataloging-in-Publication Data

Kostelni, Dolores.
  51 fast and fun slow cooker recipes / by Dolores Kostelni. -- 1st American ed.
     p. cm.
  Includes index
  ISBN 1-933112-21-2 (softcover : alk. paper)
  1. Electric cookery, Slow. 2. Quick and easy cookery. I. Title. II.
Title: Fifty-one fast and fun slow cooker recipes.
  TX827.K67 2006
  641.5'884--dc22

                            2006011341

Distributed by Publishers Group West
ISBN 10: 1-933112-21-2
ISBN 13: 978-1-933112-21-3

First American Edition
Printed in Malaysia
9 8 7 6 5 4 3 2 1

Table of Contents

Introduction

The slow cooker became an overnight sensation when the Rival Corporation introduced its Crock-Pot to the American home cook in the 1970s. Crock-Pot, the name patented by Rival, answered the call of many concerned homemakers during an energy crisis gripping the nation. Women responded to escalating inflation and higher costs by leaving the kitchen to join the work force, but their families still required proper nourishment. Eating out was not feasible; it was a time for economic restraint.

The answer was in the form of slow cooking. Trustworthy and self-sufficient, orange and avocado green Crock-Pots could burble away in America's kitchens all day, unattended, while cooking dinner to specs. This ingenious invention, with its wrap-around heating elements and heavy ceramic cooking pot, eliminated chances of food burning on the bottom and used minimal electricity—no more than that used by a 75- or 100-watt light bulb. It also adapted to different situations with a built-in timer that could be set to automatically turn off. Tenderizing tough pieces of meat—like shoulder, arm, and shank roasts—as it self-basted foods with droplets of condensation from its cover, the slow cooker was an immediate cooking phenomenon.

Interest in the slow cooker took a downward turn when the financial system stabilized and the average family's stringent cost-cutting measures loosened. Trends toward fine, home-cooked cuisine began sprouting up throughout the country, with cooking schools and television shows encouraging homemakers to be adventuresome with ingredients, to learn new techniques, and to treat their families to different, more exciting meals. The slow cooker lost its favored place in the kitchen to variations of the quick sauté and deglaze.

Twenty years later, at the cusp of the twenty-first century, a renaissance in slow cooking has taken place. This remarkable newfound interest has given rise to a new generation of slow cooker devotees who use the same type of pot with the same simple design—two or four basic settings: On and Off; or High, Low, Warm, and Off. Some models have a browning unit and a built-in timer, but to this day, there's no chance of burning the meal.

Making life and slow cooking a little easier, new slow cooker liners—plastic bags that fit into the pot—eliminate messy soaking and clean-ups. Non-stick foil liners and just plain old heavy-duty aluminum foil can assist in the same fashion while allowing foods to be lifted out of the pot using "foil handles," a definite benefit when cooking lasagna and meat loaf. Plastic liners cannot support this motion and require complete cooling before being removed from the pot.

51 Fast & Fun Slow Cooker Recipes offers an array of delicious and interesting dishes ranging from breakfast, lunch, and dinner to appetizers and desserts—a global collection of culinary delights. With recipes like Cuban Black Bean and Pork Stew and Italian Pot Roast, the slow cooker's moist heat embraces the predictably chewy cuts of beef, pork, and venison and transforms them into tender, flavorful meals. Beyond this, the slow cooker creates a balanced environment for cooking seafood—such as salmon fillet—perfectly. And forget

your past troubles with making Osso Buco, the festive Italian dish of veal shanks; with the slow cooker it's guaranteed tender and flavorful.

For desserts, a smooth cheesecake cooks up beautifully, Chocolate Spoon Cake makes its own fudge sauce, and Creamy Rice Pudding brings home a comforting, traditional dish. You'll find recipes for every occasion—whether casual, elegant, or potluck—and dish preparation is always under 20 minutes!

Today's newest home cooks are sophisticated multi-taskers, and they've rediscovered their mother's best friend in the kitchen, the slow cooker, embracing its capacity to present unfailingly delicious dinners every night. *51 Fast & Fun Slow Cooker Recipes* treats you to dishes from around the world and our own great land, with satisfying meals for every day of the week.

Tips for Success

1. Brown ground meats on the stove and drain any fat before adding to the slow cooker. Do this preparation the night before or whenever there's time before assembling the remaining ingredients in the slow cooker.

2. An option to consider if time permits is to brown roasts before adding them to the slow cooker. This extra step imparts rich flavor to the finished dish and can even be done the night before; just refrigerate the roast. Otherwise, roll the meat in seasoned flour and place in the cooker.

3. Brown chicken parts before adding them to the slow cooker to produce visually appealing, full-flavored dishes. Expedite the process by doing it the night before and refrigerating the chicken in the slow cooker pot.

4. Most milk products, such as milk, cream, and sour cream, tend to curdle during cooking. Instead, use evaporated milk for savory dishes or condensed milk for sweet dishes.

5. Buy a slow cooker with a see-through lid so you don't have to lift the lid to see what's going on. Each lift lengthens the cooking time by 15 to 30 minutes.

6. Unless specified in a recipe, stirring is unnecessary for slow cooker dishes.

7. For best results, food should come up to the halfway mark in the slow cooker pot.

8. Avoid overfilling the slow cooker pot with liquid: two-thirds to three-quarters full is a good rule of thumb. Liquids tend to spill out of an overly full cooker and they can stain the electrical base.

9. When the slow cooker cooks food, moisture accumulates on the inside of the cover and drips down into the pot, basting the ingredients and increasing the quantity of liquid in the pot. When adapting a favorite recipe to the slow cooker, use less than half the liquid originally called for.

10. If your sauce requires thickening at the end of slow cooking, stir in about 1/4 cup instant potato flakes for an easy, foolproof gravy. Or remove the meat or poultry from the pot, place a sheet of foil over the cover, set the heat on high, and wait for the liquid to come to a vigorous boil. Remove the foil and the cover, and let the sauce boil until the sauce is reduced.

11. Spray the inside of the slow cooker pot with nonstick cooking spray before adding ingredients to make clean-up easier. Using a specifically designed plastic liner or shaping heavy-duty aluminum foil to fit inside the pot is another way to easy cleaning.

12. Spots that form on the pot lining come out if you use light pressure and scrub with a multipurpose no-scratch pad and detergent.

13. The stoneware pot will crack if exposed to dramatic changes in temperature. Allow the hot pot to cool before adding cold water to it. Avoid placing the hot pot on a cold surface or on a hot stove burner. Instead, place it on heatproof mats or terry-cloth towels.

14. Root vegetables take more time to cook than meats or poultry. Place root vegetables on the bottom of the pot and the meat on top to ensure that all the ingredients cook evenly.

15. Take advantage of convenience frozen foods such as chopped onions and sliced bell peppers. Request the meat butcher in your supermarket to cut pieces of selected lean meat into small cubes or thin strips for your slow cooker dishes.

16. Give foods a burst of heat to get the cooking started: set the temperature to high for 1 hour, and then reduce to low for the remainder of the cooking time minus 1 hour.

17. To speed the heating and to raise the temperature evenly, place a sheet of aluminum foil over the slow cooker cover. Depending on what is in the pot, the foil can reduce cooking time by as much as 2 hours.

Breakfast

A breakfast revolution occurred in America during the 1970s, as more women entered the workforce, leaving them little time to make hearty, old-fashioned breakfasts. Producers of ready-to-eat cereals rose to the occasion and developed hundreds of products that encouraged quick meals and eating on the go. But as parents became more aware of nutrition and its application to the family diet, the traditional homemade breakfast began to be revived. Instead of fast foods, slow and steady cooking with the slow cooker led to the rediscovery of delicious homemade breakfasts. These recipes offer tasty opportunities to provide nourishment without spending hours at the stove.

Overnight Oatmeal

Oatmeal qualifies as a nutrient-dense cereal because it contains more protein, polyunsaturated and monounsaturated fats, minerals, and vitamins than other cereal. Another potential benefit is that oatmeal may reduce cholesterol if eaten on a regular basis.

1 1/3 cups old-fashioned rolled oats
Pinch of salt
3 cups cold water
1 tablespoon olive oil or unsalted butter

1. Gloss the pot of a 1 1/2-quart slow cooker with nonstick cooking spray or use a slow cooker liner.

2. Combine the oats, salt, water, and oil or butter in the pot of the slow cooker. Cover, set the heat on low, and cook for 8 to 9 hours or overnight. (The slow cooker should switch to the warm setting automatically once it completes its set cooking time.)

3. Stir to mix before ladling into bowls.

Overnight Oatmeal with Brown Rice

1 cup old-fashioned rolled oats
3 tablespoons brown rice
Pinch of salt
3 cups cold water
1 tablespoon olive oil or unsalted butter

Use these proportions to make oatmeal with Irish or steel-cut oats which are also known as pin-head oats because of their nubbin shape. Or omit the rice to incorporate another grain of choice, such as grits or cream of wheat.

1. Gloss the pot of a 1 1/2-quart slow cooker with nonstick cooking spray or use a slow cooker liner.

2. Combine the oats, rice, salt, water, and oil or butter in the pot of the slow cooker. Cover, set the heat on low, and cook for 8 to 9 hours or overnight. (The slow cooker should switch to the warm setting automatically once it completes its set cooking time.)

3. Stir to mix before ladling into bowls.

Overnight Scramble Casserole

Serves about 12

This delightful dish treats overnight guests to a hearty main course the next morning. Layers of potatoes, ham, cheese, and eggs marry beautifully to create a delectable dish. To serve your family this nourishing recipe, just halve the ingredients.

1. Gloss the pot of a 5- to 6-quart slow cooker with nonstick cooking spray or use a slow cooker liner.

2. Pour the frozen potatoes into a large bowl and combine with the onion and scallions. Arrange 3 1/4 cups of potato mixture in the bottom of the slow cooker. Place a few slices of ham over the potatoes. Combine the Cheddar cheese with the mozzarella and parsley. Sprinkle 1 1/2 cups of cheese over the ham. Continue alternating the layers of potatoes, ham, and cheese in the slow cooker, patting and smoothing each layer as you go, finishing with the cheese.

3. Combine the eggs, milk, salt, and pepper in a blender. Process until smooth. Pour over the ingredients in the slow cooker. Cover and refrigerate at this point, if desired, or cover and set the heat on low and cook for 8 to 9 hours.

4. Just before serving, place the large pieces of the bacon on top of the casserole and serve hot.

1 (30.5-ounce) bag frozen shredded hash brown potatoes
1 medium onion, chopped
3 scallions, ends trimmed, sliced
9 ounces thinly sliced or shaved deli ham
2 cups shredded Cheddar cheese (8 ounces)
1 cup shredded mozzarella cheese (4 ounces)
1/2 cup chopped fresh parsley leaves
12 large eggs
1 cup evaporated milk
1 teaspoon salt
1 teaspoon black pepper
1 pound sliced bacon, cooked until crisp

Cream Cheese–Stuffed Cinnamon Turnovers

3 tablespoons unsalted
  butter
1/3 cup sugar
1 tablespoon ground
  cinnamon
1 (10-count) can buttermilk
  biscuits
10 tablespoons cream
  cheese
1/3 to 1/2 cup tightly packed
  light brown sugar
Confectioners' sugar
  (optional)

These little turnovers with a cream cheese filling are given a pleasant sweetness from being rolled in cinnamon and sugar and sprinkled with brown sugar. They are also child's play to make.

1. Gloss the pot of a 3 1/2- to 4-quart slow cooker with nonstick cooking spray or use a slow cooker liner. Melt the butter in a dessert dish. Combine the sugar and cinnamon on waxed paper.

2. Separate the biscuits to make 20 round halves and flatten slightly. Place 1 1/2 teaspoons cream cheese in the center of each biscuit and fold over, pinching the edges together. Dip both sides of the turnovers in the butter, and then roll in the cinnamon and sugar. Arrange the turnovers in the bottom of the pot in one or two layers. Pour any remaining butter and cinnamon mixture over the turnovers. Sprinkle the brown sugar over the turnovers. Cover, set the heat on high, and cook for 2 to 2 1/2 hours or until a toothpick inserted in a few comes out clean.

3. Serve the turnovers from the cooker using a spoon and fork. Sift with confectioners' sugar, if desired.

Apple and Raisin-Filled Bread Pudding

Old-fashioned and homey, this beautiful bread pudding makes a fitting breakfast any day of the week, as well as a magnificent brunch buffet item. The apple pie filling makes the preparation easy.

1. Gloss the pot of a 5-quart slow cooker with nonstick cooking spray or use a slow cooker liner. Generously spread melted butter over the bottom of the pot or liner. Distribute the brown sugar over the butter. Toss the bread quarters with the remaining butter, sugar, cinnamon, and raisins, if using, in a medium bowl.

2. Place half the bread combination in the slow cooker, allowing the sugar and raisins to fall onto the bread. Distribute the apple pie filling over the bread; remove some of the thickening, if desired. Place the remaining bread over the apples, pressing down to compact the layers.

3. Whisk the eggs with the milk, vanilla, and zest. Pour the egg mixture evenly over the bread. Press down on the layers using a spatula. Cover, set the heat on low, and cook for 6 hours, or cook on high for 2 1/2 to 3 hours.

4. Serve the bread pudding from the slow cooker using large spoons.

3 tablespoons unsalted butter, melted
3/4 cup tightly packed light brown sugar
8 to 10 slices raisin, white, or whole wheat bread, cut into quarters
1/4 cup sugar
1 teaspoon ground cinnamon
1/3 cup raisins (optional)
1 (20-ounce) can apple pie filling
3 large eggs, lightly beaten
1 1/2 cups evaporated milk
1 teaspoon vanilla extract
Zest of 1 orange

FAST 51 & FUN

Appetizers

The entire world loves appetizers, especially dips and their accompanying finger-food morsels: colorful fresh vegetables, thin pieces of bread, and crackers and scoops. Attractive appetizers set the scene, whether as the prelude to dinner or as a light meal before the theater or concert, or as the casual first course at a backyard barbecue. These scrumptious slow cooker appetizers are a cinch to put together using ordinary supermarket ingredients. Your guests will love them!

Seasoned Spinach Dip

Here's a tasty dip that's a perennial favorite at parties. Ordinary ingredients— spinach, cream cheese, Parmesan cheese, and mozzarella cheese, plus the unifying mayonnaise, come together in perfect harmony.

1. Gloss the pot of a 1 1/2- to 3-quart slow cooker with nonstick cooking spray or use a slow cooker liner.

2. Mash the cream cheese in a medium bowl with 3/4 cup mayonnaise, cheeses, scallions, Italian seasoning, pepper, cayenne pepper, and spinach using a wooden spoon to combine well. Use additional mayonnaise if the mixture is not creamy enough.

3. Transfer the mixture to the slow cooker. Cover, set the heat on high, and cook for 1 1/2 to 2 1/2 hours, or cook on low for 4 to 6 hours. Stir before serving from the pot.

1 (3-ounce) package cream cheese with chives, softened

3/4 to 1 cup mayonnaise

3/4 cup grated Parmesan cheese

1/3 cup shredded mozzarella cheese

3 scallions, ends trimmed, minced

1 teaspoon dried Italian seasoning

1/4 teaspoon black pepper

Pinch of cayenne pepper

1 (10-ounce) package frozen chopped spinach, thawed and squeezed dry

Favorite chips or sliced veggies, to serve

Creamy Sausage Dip

3/4 pound ground beef
1 (16-ounce) tube hot, medium, or unseasoned breakfast sausage
1 (10 3/4-ounce) can cream of mushroom soup
3 scallions, ends trimmed, thinly sliced
1 (16-ounce) jar picante sauce
6 to 8 cups shredded Mexican 4-cheese blend (24 to 32 ounces)
Sliced French bread, favorite chips, or sliced veggies, to serve

Surprising combinations of everyday ingredients—beef, sausage, canned soup, and picante sauce—are blended here to produce this delightful dip. Regulate the spicy heat quotient by using mild picante sauce and medium or unseasoned sausage.

1. Gloss the pot of a 3 1/2- to 4-quart slow cooker with nonstick cooking spray or use a slow cooker liner.

2. Cook the beef and sausage together in a large skillet over medium heat, breaking the large pieces into crumbles with a wooden spoon. Drain the meat in a strainer and pat with paper towels to eliminate excess fat. (This step can be done the night before and refrigerated to save time.)

3. Place the meat in the pot and add the soup, scallions, picante sauce, and cheese; combine well.

4. Cover, set the heat on low, and cook for 4 to 6 hours. Stir before serving from the pot.

Ham and Bean Barbecue Dip

Serves 20

The food processor makes quick work of chopping ham and adding it to the surprise ingredients—a can of pork and beans—with barbecue sauce as the seasoning, to make this easy dip a flavor marvel.

1. Gloss the pot of a 3 1/2- to 4-quart slow cooker with nonstick cooking spray or use a slow cooker liner.

2. Add all of the ingredients to the pot, stirring to combine. Cover, set the heat on low, and cook for 4 to 6 hours, or cook on high for 2 hours. Stir before serving from the pot.

2 cups chopped cooked ham (12 ounces)

1 (11-ounce) can pork and beans

1/2 to 3/4 cup barbecue sauce of choice

3 to 5 tablespoons water

1 tablespoon brown sugar

1 teaspoon cider vinegar

1 teaspoon Worcestershire sauce

Small soft buns, sturdy chips, or French bread slices, to serve

Spicy Italian Meatballs

1 (26-ounce) jar tomato
and basil sauce
1 teaspoon dried Italian
seasoning
1 garlic clove, finely
minced
1/4 teaspoon hot pepper
flakes or hot sauce, to
taste
2 tablespoons minced fresh
parsley leaves
1 (25 1/2-ounce) bag frozen
Italian-seasoned cocktail
meatballs
French bread slices, to
serve

This popular combination doesn't get any easier because it uses frozen meatballs and your favorite jarred tomato sauce. Use these meatballs as a filling for sandwiches, too.

1. Gloss the pot of a 3 1/2- to 4-quart slow cooker with nonstick cooking spray or use a slow cooker liner.

2. Add the sauce, Italian seasoning, garlic, hot pepper flakes, and parsley to the pot and stir well. Add the meatballs, stirring to coat with sauce. Cover, set the heat on low, and cook for 6 to 7 hours, or cook on high for 3 to 4 hours.

3. Stir before serving from the pot.

Fiesta Cheese Dip

Add smoky flavor to this dip with a chopped chipotle chile. Chipotle chiles are dried and smoked jalapeños that are sold canned in a thick adobo sauce, which is seasoned with vinegar and spices.

1. Gloss the pot of a 3 1/2- to 4-quart slow cooker with nonstick cooking spray or use a slow cooker liner.

2. Add the onion, salsa, Worcestershire sauce, cheeses, and beer to the pot, stirring to combine. Cover, set the heat on low, and cook for 4 to 5 hours, or cook on high for 2 to 3 hours.

3. Stir the ingredients and serve directly from the pot with plenty of chips and dippers.

1 small onion, finely minced

1 (16-ounce) jar salsa or taco sauce

1 teaspoon Worcestershire sauce

4 cups cubed processed cheese (about 1 pound)

1 1/2 cups shredded sharp Cheddar or Mexican-style cheese (6 ounces)

1/2 to 3/4 cup beer or evaporated milk

Tortilla chips and dippers, to serve

Hot Crab Dip

Serves 10 to 12

This combination of ingredients is one of the best dips ever devised. Introduced in the 1950s when dips were the "in" party food, its popularity continues. For more zip, double the horseradish and hot sauce.

1 (8-ounce) package cream cheese, softened, cut into small pieces
1 tablespoon Worcestershire sauce
1/2 cup mayonnaise
8 ounces lump crab meat, drained, juice reserved, picked over for cartilage
1 scallion, trimmed, finely sliced
1 teaspoon minced dried onion

2 teaspoons minced garlic
1/2 teaspoon creamy horseradish, or to taste
1 tablespoon lime juice
Dash of hot sauce
2 tablespoons finely minced fresh parsley or fresh cilantro leaves
Crackers, small French bread slices, or celery, to serve

1. Gloss the pot of a 1 1/2-quart slow cooker with nonstick cooking spray or use a slow cooker liner.

2. Mix the cream cheese, Worcestershire sauce, mayonnaise, crab meat, scallion, onion, garlic, horseradish, lime juice, and hot sauce in the pot. Cover, set the heat on low, and cook for 2 to 3 1/2 hours or until the dip is creamy. Stir once or twice to ensure the dip is blended.

3. Stir in the parsley or cilantro before serving, with crackers, bread slices, or celery.

Chili-Bean Dip

1 large onion, chopped
2 (15-ounce) cans tomato
sauce
2 (16-ounce) cans kidney
beans, drained
1 (6-ounce) can tomato
paste
1 1/2 cups water
1 cup beer
3 tablespoons chili powder
1 teaspoon brown sugar
2 tablespoons olive oil
1 1/2 to 2 pounds ground
beef
Corn chips and dippers, to
serve

Everyone anticipates this great chili-bean dip during football playoffs or as an entrée with cornbread for casual meals. This flexible recipe also works with ground venison combined with beef and pork sausage for another flavor dimension.

1. Gloss the pot of a 5-quart slow cooker with nonstick cooking spray or use a slow cooker liner.

2. Place the onion, tomato sauce, beans, tomato paste, water, beer, chili powder, and brown sugar in the pot. Cover and set the heat on low.

3. Warm the oil in a large skillet and brown the beef until no longer pink, about 5 minutes; stir to break up the large pieces. Drain the beef in a colander to eliminate excess fat. Transfer the meat to the slow cooker and stir to combine. (This step can also be done the night before and refrigerated.)

4. Cover and cook on low for 6 to 7 hours, or cook on high for 4 hours. Serve hot from the slow cooker and offer plenty of chips and scoops.

Bagna Cauda—
Hot Oil Vegetable Dip

This simple oil and butter sauce seasoned with garlic and anchovies is a specialty of the Piedmont region of Italy. The name means "hot bath," and it's the perfect dip for fresh vegetables. Serve this with a rustic red wine.

1. Melt the butter with the oil and garlic in the pot of a 1 1/2-quart slow cooker with the heat set on high for about 1 hour.

2. Set the heat on low, add the anchovies, and stir vigorously with a wooden spoon to incorporate. Season to taste with the black pepper. Continue to cook on low for 1 to 2 hours.

3. Stir in parsley just before serving. Serve hot from the slow cooker with the cut vegetables alongside.

1 cup (2 sticks) unsalted
   butter
1/2 to 2/3 cup olive oil
2 tablespoons minced
   garlic
4 anchovy fillets, well
   rinsed, patted dry, and
   finely chopped
Freshly ground black
   pepper
1/4 cup chopped fresh
   parsley
Sliced fresh vegetables
   such as fennel, celery,
   red pepper, plus whole
   grape tomatoes, baby
   artichokes, or raw, thin
   asparagus spears

Soups

Soups take little time to put together, and they arrive at the table full of fragrant broth and wholesome ingredients. Soup also puts to tasty use some miscellaneous items you may have accumulated over time, whether pasta, dried beans, or chunks of Parmesan cheese—all of which add seasoning and help thicken soups to a hearty brew. Soup is a favorite all over the world, and these recipes reflect typical flavors of Mexico, Italy, Greece, and our own country, America. Similar ingredients are used throughout the world, but the seasonings make them unique to particular countries.

Red Lentil and Split Pea Soup

Serves about 10

The combination of red lentils and green split peas makes for a snappy, bright soup, but you can use only one type of bean, if preferred. Red lentils are available at health food and gourmet stores.

1. Combine the lentils, split peas, ham bone, onions, carrots, celery, bay leaf, and peppercorns in a 5- to 7-quart slow cooker. Cover the ingredients with water. Sprinkle the bouillon cubes over the ingredients. Cover, set the heat on low, and cook for 7 to 8 hours, or cook on high for 4 to 6 hours, until the soup is thickened and the ingredients are tender.

2. Remove the ham bone from the soup with a slotted spoon. When cool enough to handle, pick off all the meat and place it back in the slow cooker, stirring to incorporate.

3. Remove bay leaf before serving hot from the slow cooker into deep soup bowls.

1/2 pound red lentils, sorted, well rinsed

1/2 pound green split peas, sorted, well rinsed

1 (about 1 1/2 pounds) ham bone or ham hock with meat

2 large onions, minced

3 large carrots, peeled, trimmed, sliced

2 medium celery stalks with leaves, sliced

1 bay leaf

Several black peppercorns

Water

4 chicken bouillon cubes, crushed

Macaroni and 3-Bean Soup

1 large onion, chopped
1 large or 3 small to
  medium garlic cloves
2 medium carrots, peeled,
  trimmed, sliced
2 medium celery ribs,
  thinly sliced
1 (16-ounce) can great
  northern or cannellini
  beans, drained, rinsed
1 (16-ounce) can red
  kidney beans, drained,
  rinsed
1 (10-ounce) package
  frozen lima beans
1 (10 3/4-ounce) can
  tomato soup
5 vegetable or chicken
  bouillon cubes, crumbled
1 tablespoon dried Italian
  seasoning

1 bay leaf
2 tablespoons olive oil
Pinch of hot pepper flakes
6 cups water
1/4 to 1/3 cup broken and
  assorted pastas
Chopped fresh parsley, to
  serve

This nutritious and attractive soup takes no time to put together and it arrives at the table full of fragrant broth, beans, and vegetables.

1. Combine the onion, garlic, carrots, and celery in a 5- to 6-quart slow cooker. Add the great northern, red kidney, and lima beans, along with the tomato soup. Sprinkle the bouillon cubes over the ingredients and stir in the Italian seasoning, bay leaf, oil, hot pepper flakes, and water.

2. Cover, set the heat on low, and cook for 6 to 7 hours, or cook on high for 3 to 4 hours. One hour before the end of cooking time, stir in the pasta. Cover and cook 1 hour.

3. Remove the bay leaf and discard. Garnish with the parsley, and serve hot in deep soup bowls.

Southwestern Pork and White Bean Soup

A successful marriage of ingredients takes place in this hearty stew, with cumin zipping up the flavor. Use your favorite white beans in this soup; they all produce delectable results.

1. Place the beans in a 3 1/2- to 4-quart slow cooker and set the heat on high.

2. Warm the oil over medium-high heat in a large skillet. Sauté the pork, onion, and garlic until the onions soften and the pork loses its raw, pink look. Turn off the heat and stir in the jalapeño, cumin, and chili powder. Add the mixture to the slow cooker and stir into the beans. Pour in the water and stir in the crushed bouillon cubes. Cover and cook on low for 4 to 5 hours, until the pork is tender.

3. Before serving, stir in the cilantro. Serve in deep soup bowls. You can add hot rice to each bowl if you wish to make the stew thicker, or serve the rice on the side

2 (16-ounce) cans white beans, such as navy, great northern, or cannellini, drained, rinsed

1 tablespoon olive oil

1 1/2 pounds boneless pork, trimmed of fat, cut into 1-inch strips

1 medium onion, thinly sliced

1 large garlic clove, minced

2 tablespoons diced jalapeño chili pepper

1 teaspoon ground cumin

1/4 teaspoon chili powder

3 cups water

3 chicken bouillon cubes, crushed

Chopped fresh cilantro, to serve

Hot rice, to serve

Escarole and Chicken Soup

3 cups cubed, diced, or torn
cooked chicken
4 cups water
1 (.9-ounce) envelope dry
vegetable soup mix
1 (14 1/2-ounce) can
chicken broth
3 medium carrots,
peeled, trimmed, sliced
2 bunches curly or plain
escarole, washed,
snipped into small pieces
1 1/2 cups cooked rice or
small pasta
Grated Parmesan cheese,
to serve

This is an easy way to make a wonderful homemade soup using chicken, pasta, and escarole, a lettuce used as a cooked vegetable in Mediterranean cuisines.

1. Place the chicken in a 5- to 6-quart slow cooker and add the water. Stir in the soup mix, chicken broth, carrots, and escarole. Cover, set the heat on low, and cook for 6 to 8 hours, until the broth is golden and the ingredients are tender.

2. Stir in the cooked rice or pasta.

3. Serve the soup hot in deep soup bowls with generous helpings of Parmesan cheese.

Beef and Vegetable Soup

The slow cooker excels at making wonderful one-dish meals, and this hearty soup is one of those. Add your favorite vegetables, too.

1. Place the potatoes, onions, carrots, and celery on the bottom of a 5- to 6-quart slow cooker. Place the meat on top of the vegetables.

2. Add the water, tomatoes, bouillon cubes, ketchup, bay leaf, and barley, stirring to combine. Cover, set the heat on low, and cook for 7 to 8 hours, or cook on high for 4 to 5 hours.

3. Remember to remove the bay leaf from the soup. Stir before serving and ladle into deep soup bowls.

3 medium Yukon Gold
   potatoes, cubed
2 medium onions, chopped
3 large carrots, peeled,
   trimmed, sliced
3 medium celery stalks with
   leaves, sliced
1 pound stew beef, cut
   into 1/2-inch cubes
3 cups water
1 (14.5-ounce) cans diced
   tomatoes
5 beef bouillon cubes,
   crushed
1/3 cup ketchup
1 bay leaf
1/3 cup pearled barley

Mexican-Style Tomato-Tortilla Soup

2 tablespoons olive oil
1 medium onion, chopped
1 garlic clove, minced
1 (26-ounce) can tomato
    soup
1 (14.5-ounce) can stewed
    tomatoes, crushed
1 tablespoon diced
    jalapeño chile pepper,
    rinsed
2 to 4 tablespoons salsa of
    choice
1 teaspoon ground cumin
2 cups water
4 chicken or vegetable
    bouillon cubes, crushed

1/2 teaspoon dried
    Mexican oregano
Pinch of cayenne pepper
Several sprigs of cilantro,
    chopped
6 to 8 small soft corn
    tortillas
Olive oil
Salt
Juice of 1 lime
Sour cream, shredded
    Cheddar cheese,
    chopped avocado,
    to garnish

Variations of this Tex-Mex soup abound. This thoroughly delicious tomato version presents opportunities for enrichment with the addition of cooked meat or chicken. Use tortilla chips instead of the tortilla strips, if preferred.

1. Gloss the inside of a 4- to 6-quart slow cooker with cooking spray. Spread the oil in the bottom of the slow cooker.

2. Add the onion, garlic, tomato soup, stewed tomatoes, jalapeño, salsa, cumin, water, bouillon cubes, oregano, and cayenne pepper to the slow cooker. Stir to combine the ingredients. Cover, set the heat on high, and cook for 1 hour. Then set the heat on low and cook for 4 to 5 hours.

3. While the soup cooks, prepare the tortilla strips. Preheat the oven to 350°F. Stack the tortillas and cut into 1/4- to 1/2-inch strips. Scatter over a large baking pan, drizzle with a little olive oil, and sprinkle lightly with salt. Bake until crisp and beginning to turn golden brown around the edges, about 15 minutes. Set aside to cool.

4. Just before serving the soup, add the lime juice. Arrange the sour cream, shredded cheese, chopped avocado, and tortilla strips in small dishes on a tray. Ladle the hot soup into deep bowls, sprinkle with the cilantro and a few tortilla strips, and pass the condiments.

Greek Bean Soup

2 (16-ounce) cans cannellini
  or great northern beans,
  drained, rinsed
1 (14.5-ounce) can stewed
  tomatoes, crushed
1/4 cup olive oil
1 tablespoon minced garlic
1/2 cup sliced celery
1 teaspoon dried oregano
1 teaspoon dried thyme
1 bay leaf
1/2 cup dry white wine
6 cups water
3 tablespoons white rice
Crumbled feta cheese, to
  garnish
Sliced Kalamata olives, to
  garnish

*This soup incorporates many Mediterranean ingredients such as beans,
tomatoes, garlic, olives, feta cheese, and olive oil. Bread makes
the perfect accompaniment to this hearty, robust dish.*

1. Place the beans, tomatoes, oil, garlic, celery, oregano, thyme, bay leaf, wine, water, and rice in a 5- to 6-quart slow cooker. Cover, set the heat on low, and cook for 6 to 7 hours, or cook on high for 4 to 5 hours.

2. Stir soup and remove the bay leaf. Serve hot from the pot ladling into deep soup bowls. Garnish with feta cheese and olives.

Hungarian Goulash Soup

This Hungarian soup is a stew composed of many ingredients, which explains the name "goulash."

1. Place the potatoes, beef, drippings or oil, onions, garlic, caraway seeds, paprika, and tomatoes in the pot of a 5- to 6-quart slow cooker. Stir in enough cold water to cover the solid ingredients and sprinkle the bouillon cubes over the water.

2. Cover, set the heat on low, and cook for 6 to 8 hours, or cook on high for 4 to 5 hours, until the meat is tender.

3. Serve hot from the pot, ladling into deep soup bowls. Serve with crusty bread.

2 pounds potatoes, cubed
1 1/2 pounds cubed lean beef, rinsed, drained
1/4 cup bacon drippings or olive oil
2 large onions, finely chopped
1 large garlic clove, crushed
1/2 teaspoon caraway seeds
1 1/2 teaspoons paprika
1 (16-ounce) can stewed tomatoes, crushed
Water
8 beef bouillon cubes, crushed

Minestrone

Minestrone translates from Italian to mean "a big, thick vegetable soup." Add whatever vegetables you have on hand to make it your own: that's the Italian way.

5 chicken or vegetable bouillon cubes

4 cups hot water

1 medium onion, thinly sliced

2 medium celery ribs, sliced

2 garlic cloves, minced

1 cup frozen or fresh-cut green beans

5 medium carrots, peeled, trimmed, sliced

1 small cabbage head, quartered, cored, thinly sliced (about 2 cups)

2 (14.5-ounce) cans stewed tomatoes, crushed

2 medium red potatoes, cut into eighths

1 (16-ounce) can cannellini, great northern, or navy beans, drained, rinsed

1 bay leaf

3 tablespoons olive oil

1/4 cup elbow macaroni, cooked al dente (optional)

Freshly grated Parmesan cheese, to garnish

1. Dissolve the bouillon cubes in the hot water and set aside.

2. Place the onion, celery, garlic, green beans, carrots, cabbage, tomatoes, potatoes, beans, and bay leaf in the pot of a 5- to 6-quart slow cooker. Pour the bouillon over the solid ingredients. If the solids are not covered, add more water. Stir in the oil.

3. Cover, set the heat on low, and cook for 6 to 7 hours. Thirty minutes before cooking time is completed, stir in the macaroni. Cover and cook for 30 minutes.

4. Remove the bay leaf from the soup before serving hot from the slow cooker. Ladle into deep soup bowls and pass the Parmesan.

FAST 51 & FUN

Beef, Lamb, and Venison

Meat makes the meal. Celebration tables are always laden with good, old-fashioned meat dishes and favorite comfort foods. Pot roast brings hearty meat and vegetable flavors to a meal, especially if time permits browning the meat before braising it in a seasoned liquid. Meat loaf epitomizes comfort food, and simple components yield spectacular results. The magic of the slow cooker transforms chewy meats, such as the increasingly popular venison, into fork-tender meals.

Meat Loaf with Roasted Tomatoes

Serves 6 to 8

Use an oval slow cooker, if possible, for this meat loaf. A slow cooker's heating element is located in the side of the outside container, so by placing the tomatoes along the side, they get the full benefit of the heat and will "roast."

1. Line the pot of a 3 1/2- to 4-quart slow cooker with crossed pieces of heavy-duty aluminum foil and gloss with nonstick cooking spray.

2. In a large bowl, combine the meats, onion, garlic, bread crumbs, eggs, 1/3 cup of soup, parsley, salt, and pepper, and toss lightly to combine. Shape the meat to fit in the slow cooker and place inside.

3. Cut the tomatoes in half and place around the sides of the meat loaf. Spoon the remaining tomato soup over the meat loaf. Combine the ketchup and mustard, and spread over the top of the meat loaf. Cover, set the heat on low, and cook for 5 to 6 hours, or cook on high for 3 to 4 hours.

4. Turn the slow cooker off and uncover. Allow the meat loaf to sit in the pot about 15 minutes.

5. Remove the meat loaf from the cooker using the foil to lift it out. Cut the meat loaf into thick slices and place a roasted tomato on each slice. Serve hot.

1 pound ground beef
1/2 pound ground pork
1/2 cup finely chopped onion
2 garlic cloves, minced
1 1/2 cups Italian-seasoned dried bread crumbs
2 large eggs, slightly beaten
1 (10 3/4-ounce) can condensed tomato soup
1/3 cup chopped fresh parsley
1 teaspoon salt
Dash of black pepper
1 (14.5-ounce) can whole tomatoes, drained
1/4 cup ketchup
1 teaspoon dry mustard

Beef Pot Roast with Vegetables

4 medium carrots, peeled, trimmed, cut into 2-inch pieces

4 medium Yukon Gold potatoes, peeled, cut into quarters

2 medium onions, cut into quarters

1 large garlic clove, sliced

1 to 3 tablespoons olive oil

1/4 cup all-purpose flour

1/2 teaspoon salt

1/2 teaspoon black pepper

1/2 teaspoon dried thyme

1/2 teaspoon paprika

1/4 teaspoon garlic salt

3- to 4-pound boneless chuck roast, rolled, tied

1 (10 3/4-ounce) can condensed cream of mushroom soup

1 (1-ounce) envelope dry onion soup mix

The slow cooker is a perfect pot to produce this wonderfully tender pot roast. This dish is equally at home with both company and family.

1. Gloss a 5- to 6-quart slow cooker with nonstick cooking spray or use a slow cooker liner.

2. Combine the carrots, potatoes, onions, and garlic with 1 tablespoon of oil in the bottom of the slow cooker. Cover and set the heat on low.

3. Combine the flour, salt, pepper, thyme, paprika, and garlic salt on a piece of wax paper. Roll the beef in the seasoned flour until coated well.

4. If time permits, brown the beef in the remaining oil. If time is short, place the beef on top of the vegetables.

5. Mix the mushroom soup and onion soup mix. Pour the combined soups over the meat. Cover and cook on low for 6 to 7 hours, or cook on high for 3 to 4 hours. Transfer the meat to a cutting board and allow it to rest for 15 minutes.

6. Remove the string. Cut the meat into 1/2-inch slices and arrange overlapping on a platter. Place the vegetables and gravy in a serving dish. Spoon some gravy over the meat and serve.

Corned Beef and Cabbage Dinner

Serves 6 to 8

Celebrate St. Patrick's Day and Irish luck with this fine meal. Corning refers to the pre-refrigeration process of preserving and seasoning meat, often brisket, with a rub of salt and spice mixture. Today, we usually buy our meat already corned.

1 (3- to 4-pound) corned
  beef brisket
4 medium potatoes,
  peeled, halved
1 (1-ounce) envelope dry
  onion soup mix
1 garlic clove, sliced
Water
1 bay leaf
1 medium green cabbage,
  cut into wedges
Various mustards of choice,
  to serve
Malt vinegar, to serve

1. Gloss the pot of a 5- to 6-quart slow cooker with nonstick cooking spray or use a slow cooker liner.

2. Rinse off the meat and pat dry with paper towels. Discard any brine from the package, but reserve the seasoning packet, if desired.

3. Place the potatoes in the bottom of the slow cooker. Place the meat on top, sprinkle with the onion soup mix, and add the garlic. Pour enough water over the meat to just cover. Place the bay leaf on the meat. Sprinkle in the seasoning packet, if using.

4. Cover, set the heat on low, and cook for 8 to 10 hours, or cook on high for 5 to 6 hours. If the cabbage fits in, add it during the last 45 minutes to 1 hour of cooking. Otherwise, transfer the meat and potatoes to a platter, cover, and keep warm; remove the bay leaf. Place the cabbage in the hot liquid. Cover and cook on high for 30 to 45 minutes or until desired doneness.

5. Slice the meat into thin pieces against the grain and arrange the slices overlapping on a platter. Surround with the potatoes, and place the cabbage in a separate bowl. Serve with various mustards and a cruet of vinegar for seasoning the cabbage.

Swiss Steak

1 1/2 to 2 pounds round
  steak, cut into 4 to
  6 pieces
1/3 cup all-purpose flour
1 1/2 teaspoons dry mustard
1 teaspoon paprika
1/2 teaspoon seasoned salt
1/4 teaspoon black pepper
3 to 4 tablespoons olive oil
  (optional)
1 (14.5-ounce) can stewed
  tomatoes, crushed
1 medium onion, cut in half,
  sliced

Called "smothered steak" in Great Britain, this usually chewy meat is cooked to a succulent tenderness in the slow cooker. This recipe easily extends upward to serve more people, and is also easily adapted for venison.

1. Pat the meat dry with paper towels. Pound it into thinner steaks using a meat mallet.

2. Combine the flour with the mustard, paprika, salt, and pepper. Dredge both sides of the steaks in the flour mixture.

3. If time permits, warm the oil in a large skillet and brown the steaks on both sides. If time is short, place the seasoned meat in the pot of a 3 1/2- to 4-quart slow cooker.

4. Add the tomatoes and onion. Cover, set the heat on low, and cook for 6 to 7 hours, or cook on high for 3 to 4 hours, until the meat is fork-tender.

5. Serve directly from the slow cooker.

Steak and Black Bean Chili

This seasoned chili combines flank steak, typical chili seasonings, and black beans for a real flavor treat. Jack up the heat with smoky chipotle chiles or diced jalapeño chile peppers. The cornmeal thickens the chili without adding flavor.

1. Place the onions, garlic, meat, chili powder, cumin, and oregano in the pot of a 5- to 6-quart slow cooker. Drizzle the oil over the ingredients. Mix to combine using your hands or two wooden spoons.

2. Add the chiles, tomatoes, tomato sauce, black beans, onion soup mix, and paprika. Whisk the cornmeal into the water until dissolved. Pour over the ingredients and stir to combine.

3. Cover, set the heat on low, and cook for 7 to 8 hours, or cook on high for 4 hours, until the meat is fork-tender and the flavors are blended.

4. Serve directly from the slow cooker.

2 large onions, chopped
2 large garlic cloves, minced
3 to 4 pounds flank steak, cut into 1- to 2-inch strips
2 tablespoons chili powder
1 teaspoon ground cumin
1 teaspoon dried Mexican oregano
3 tablespoons olive oil
1 (4-ounce) can chopped green chiles
1 (14.5-ounce) can stewed tomatoes, crushed
1 (15-ounce) can tomato sauce
2 (15-ounce) cans black beans, drained, rinsed
1 (1-ounce) envelope dry onion soup mix
1 tablespoon paprika
1/4 cup yellow cornmeal
2 cups water

Leg of Lamb with White Beans

Serves about 6

3 medium onions,
   thinly sliced
2 (16-ounce) cans white
   kidney beans, such as
   great northern or
   cannellini, drained,
   rinsed
2 (14 1/2-ounce) cans
   stewed tomatoes, crushed
2 large garlic cloves,
   minced
1 tablespoon dried
   Italian seasoning
2 to 4 tablespoons olive oil
3 pounds boneless leg of
   lamb, trimmed of
   excess fat
1/4 cup chopped fresh
   parsley

Robustly seasoned, lamb prepared in this manner makes an impressive, satisfying dinner. Lamb is usually available fresh or deep-chilled but not frozen; it should show some white fat.

1. Gloss the pot of a 5- to 6-quart slow cooker with nonstick cooking spray or use a slow cooker liner.

2. Add the onions, beans, tomatoes, garlic, and Italian seasoning to the slow cooker and mix with 2 tablespoons of the oil.

3. If time permits, warm 2 tablespoons of oil in a large skillet and brown the meat on all sides. Transfer the lamb to the slow cooker and nestle it in the beans.

4. Cover and cook on low for 6 to 7 hours, or cook on high for 4 1/2 hours.

5. If time is short, nestle the lamb in the beans. Cover and cook at low 6 to 7 hours.

6. Transfer the lamb to a cutting board and allow it to sit 15 minutes.

7. Spoon the beans into a large, deep platter. Cut the meat into 1/4- to 1/2-inch slices, and lay them overlapping on the beans. Sprinkle with chopped parsley and serve hot.

Chili con Quicko

This dish is so quick and easy to make using pantry ingredients, and the tasty results are guaranteed. Serve this chili over hot dogs and burgers, or just straight up in bowls. Venison also works well in this chili.

1. Gloss the pot of a 3 1/2- to 4-quart slow cooker with nonstick cooking spray or use a slow cooker liner.

2. Warm the oil in a large skillet over medium heat and brown the beef with the onion, breaking the meat into small pieces until it is no longer pink. Using a strainer, drain the meat of excess fat and transfer the meat to the slow cooker. (This step can be done the night before and refrigerated.)

3. Mix in the chili powder, mustard, Worcestershire sauce, salt, beans, and soup. Cover and cook on low for 4 1/2 to 5 hours, or cook on high for 3 to 4 hours.

4. Serve hot, directly from the slow cooker.

1 tablespoon olive oil
1 1/2 pounds ground beef
1/2 cup chopped onion
2 to 3 teaspoons mild chili powder
1 tablespoon prepared mustard
1 tablespoon Worcestershire sauce
1 teaspoon salt
1 (14 3/4-ounce) can baked beans in tomato sauce
1 (16-ounce) can pinto beans, drained, rinsed
1 (10 3/4-ounce) can condensed tomato soup

Italian Pot Roast

1/3 cup all-purpose flour
1 tablespoon dry Italian
salad dressing mix
(from .7-ounce envelope)
3- to 4-pound eye
round roast
3 or more tablespoons
olive oil (optional)
1/2 pound Canadian bacon
or ham, small diced
1 large onion, diced
4 large garlic cloves,
finely minced
2 large potatoes, quartered
2 large carrots, cut into
2-inch pieces
4 medium celery ribs, cut
into 2-inch pieces
1/2 cup red wine
1 cup water

*The typically chewy eye round cut of beef makes the most attractive roast,
and the slow cooker tenderizes the meat to perfection.*

1 bay leaf
4 beef bouillon cubes,
crushed
1 (10-ounce) package
frozen small peas,
thawed (optional)

1. Combine the flour and salad dressing mix on a sheet of wax paper. Roll the roast in the flour mixture.

2. Warm the oil in a large skillet and sauté the bacon or ham, onion, and garlic over medium-low heat until the bacon or ham is crisp and the onion is soft. Transfer the cooked mixture to the slow cooker pot, leaving the fat in the skillet. Place the potatoes, carrots, and celery on top of the ham mixture. If time is short, place the bacon or ham on top of the vegetables.

3. If time permits, add more oil to the skillet, if necessary. Brown the roast on all sides and place in the slow cooker on top of the vegetables. Pour the red wine into the skillet. Bring it to the boil, scrape up any brown bits sticking to the skillet, and pour the wine over the meat.

4. Add the water, bay leaf, and crushed bouillon to the slow cooker. Cover, set the heat on low, and cook for 6 to 7 hours, or cook on high for 3 to 4 hours, until the meat is fork-tender.

5. If time is short, place the roast in the slow cooker pot. Pour in the wine, water, and crushed bouillon cubes; place the bay leaf on the meat and cook for the allotted time.

6. Transfer the meat to a cutting board and allow it to sit about 15 minutes. Remove the bay leaf.

7. While the meat is resting, add the peas, if using, to the slow cooker and set on high, cover, and cook 20 minutes.

8. Slice the meat into 1/2-inch slices and place overlapping on a platter. Ladle some pea sauce over the meat; spoon the vegetables into a serving bowl, and serve.

Beef in Burgundy Wine Sauce

1/2 cup all-purpose flour

1 teaspoon dried thyme

1 teaspoon paprika

1/2 teaspoon salt, plus
more to taste

1/2 teaspoon black pepper, plus
more to taste

2 1/2 to 4 pounds beef
chuck or lean stew meat,
cut into 1-inch cubes

4 slices bacon, cooked
crisp, crumbled

1 pound sliced fresh
button mushrooms

1 pound baby carrots

2 tablespoons tomato paste

1 cup Burgundy or other
dry red wine

1 large garlic clove, minced

1 (10 3/4-ounce) can condensed
golden mushroom soup

1 (10 3/4-ounce) can condensed
beef broth

Cooked noodles, rice, or
mashed potatoes to serve

A slow cooker version of the French classic Boeuf Bourguignonne *is actually a hearty beef and wine stew with vegetables. This dish is great winter fare worthy of company and good china, even if you use precooked bacon.*

1. Spray the pot of a 5- to 6-quart slow cooker with nonstick spray or use a slow cooker liner.

2. Combine the flour with thyme, paprika, salt, and pepper on a sheet of wax paper. Roll the meat in the seasoned flour. Mix the bacon crumbles with the meat, mushrooms, and carrots in the pot. Whisk the tomato paste with the wine, garlic, and soups, and pour over the meat and vegetable mixture. Season with salt and pepper, if desired.

3. Cover and cook on low for 7 to 8 hours, or cook on high for 4 to 5 hours.

4. Serve hot over noodles, rice, or mashed potatoes.

The name osso buco means "bone with a hole" and the meat is always served with the bone. Spread the marrow on bread and season with salt and pepper for a luxurious treat. Gremolata, the lemony seasoning, brightens the flavor of the meat.

1. Gloss the pot of a 5- to 6-quart slow cooker with nonstick cooking spray or use a slow cooker liner.

2. Tie the shanks with kitchen string around their middles to keep the meat together during cooking. Combine the flour, salt and pepper on a sheet of wax paper. Roll the shanks in the seasoned flour.

3. If time permits, warm the oil with the butter in a large skillet over medium-high heat. When the butter melts, brown the shanks on both sides. Transfer the shanks to the slow cooker as they are done. Then add the onion, garlic, wine, bouillon cubes, and thyme to the slow cooker. If time is short, place the onion, garlic, veal shanks, wine, crushed bouillon, and thyme in the slow cooker.

4. Cover and cook on low for 6 to 8 hours, until the meat is fork-tender.

5. While the meat cooks, prepare the gremolata by mixing together the parsley, zest, and garlic in a bowl.

6. Place the meat on a serving platter and spoon the sauce around and over the shanks. Sprinkle with gremolata and serve.

For the shanks:

6 to 8 veal, pork, or lamb shanks

1/2 cup all-purpose flour

Salt and pepper

3 tablespoons olive oil (optional)

3 tablespoons unsalted butter (optional)

1 large onion, minced

1 tablespoon minced garlic

1 1/2 cups dry white wine

4 chicken bouillon cubes, crushed

2 teaspoons dried thyme

For the Gremolata:

3 tablespoons minced fresh parsley leaves

Zest of 1 lemon

1/2 teaspoon minced garlic

Pork, Sausages, and Ham

Today's leaner pork is different from the succulent pork of 30 years ago. Demands by consumers for lean meat triggered the production of pork with less fat and without the marbleized flesh of yesteryear. Thus, cooking can leave the meat dry, so it's essential to add flavor and tenderness with seasonings and the moisture of the slow cooker. These recipes show off pork as a versatile meat that is a mainstay during the holidays, for summer picnics, and for everyday meals.

Sicilian Sausage and Pepperoni Lasagna

Serves 6 to 8

This robustly seasoned dish of Italian sausage, pepperoni, and tomato sauce layered with lasagna noodles is a real time-saver because it uses uncooked noodles and requires only assembly of supermarket ingredients. The uncooked noodles soften as the dish cooks in the slow cooker.

1. Combine the mozzarella with the Parmesan or Asiago cheese and chopped parsley.

2. Line a 4 1/2- to 6-quart slow cooker with aluminum foil in a crisscross pattern and gloss the foil with nonstick cooking spray. Sprinkle bread crumbs over the bottom of the liner.

3. Spread 1/3 cup tomato sauce over the bread crumbs. Arrange 3 to 5 noodles over the sauce, breaking them to fit. Spread another 1/2 cup of tomato sauce over the uncooked noodles, then top with some of the pepperoni strips, sausage pieces, and cheeses. Continue in this way, alternating layers of the ingredients and ending with a top layer of cheeses.

4. Cover, set the heat on low, and cook for 2 1/2 to 3 hours or until the cheese is melted, the sides are browned, and a knife inserts easily in the center. If necessary, hold this dish on warm for 30 minutes to 1 hour.

5. Remove the lasagna from the slow cooker by lifting up on the foil. Place the lasagna on a cutting board and allow it to sit for several minutes before removing the foil and cutting into wedges. Serve hot with a salad.

3 cups shredded mozzarella cheese (12 ounces)

1 cup grated Parmesan or Asiago cheese (4 ounces)

1/3 cup chopped fresh parsley

2 tablespoons Italian-seasoned dried bread crumbs

4 cups tomato sauce

9 to 12 uncooked lasagna noodles

Several slices pepperoni, cut into strips

1 to 2 pounds cooked mild, sweet, or hot Italian link sausage, cut into 1/2-inch pieces

Sauerkraut with Sausages, Ham, and Chops

3 medium onions, quartered
2 to 3 large carrots, peeled, sliced
2 to 3 medium potatoes, peeled, quartered
4 to 6 garlic cloves, sliced
3 or more tablespoons olive oil
1 to 1 1/2 pounds whole Canadian bacon or Daisy ham
1 (19.5-ounce) package (5 large links) bratwurst sausages, pricked with a fork
6 smoked pork chops
3 bay leaves
Several whole black peppercorns
Several juniper berries
2 pounds (32 ounces) sauerkraut, rinsed
4 to 5 chicken bouillon cubes

Classically known as choucroute garni, *this Oktoberfest feast is heaped high on huge platters and is accompanied by an assortment of mustards and some crusty rye bread. Supermarkets stock juniper berries in the spice section.*

1 cup hot water
1 cup medium fruity white wine, such as Reisling

1. Place the onions, carrots, potatoes, and garlic in the bottom of a 6- to 7-quart slow cooker. Pour 1 tablespoon of the oil over the vegetables and toss until they are coated. Place the ham on top of the vegetables. Cover, set the heat on high, and begin cooking.

2. Warm the remaining 2 tablespoons oil in a large skillet over medium heat and brown the sausages (this can be done the night before as well to save time).

3. Place the sausages in the slow cooker along with the chops. Distribute the bay leaves, peppercorns, and juniper berries over the meat. Place the sauerkraut over the meats and drizzle with the oil and sausage fat remaining in the skillet.

4. Dissolve the bouillon cubes in the hot water. Pour the water along with the wine over the sauerkraut. Cover, set the heat on low, and cook for 10 to 12 hours.

5. Remove and discard bay leaves. Serve this as they do in Europe, piled on large platters with baskets of rye bread and strong mustards so everyone can help themselves.

Pork Roast Italiano

The slow cooker and seasonings help immeasurably in giving pork a succulent quality. The finishing sauce thickens and flavors the cooking liquid.

1. Score the fat on the top of the roast with a small knife in a crisscross pattern. Combine the flour with 1 tablespoon of the salad dressing mix on a sheet of wax paper and roll the pork in the seasoned flour.

2. If time permits, warm the oil in a large skillet over medium heat and brown the meat on all sides. Place the meat in a (5- to 6-quart) slow cooker. Arrange the rosemary and sage leaves on the meat, if using. If time is short, roll the pork in the seasoned flour and place in the pot of the slow cooker. Sprinkle the herbs on the meat.

3. Pour the wine and water into the slow cooker and add the remaining salad dressing mix and bouillon cubes. Cover, set the heat on low, and cook for 6 to 8 hours, or cook on high for 3 1/2 to 4 hours, until the meat is fork-tender.

4. Remove the roast from the slow cooker, place on a cutting board, and discard the herbs. Allow the roast to sit for about 15 minutes.

5. Leave the slow cooker uncovered and set the heat on high. Stir in the sauce mix or instant potato flakes and cook until thickened. Stir in the parsley.

6. Slice the pork into 1/2-inch or 1/4-inch pieces. Overlap the slices on a warmed platter. Spoon some sauce over the meat and serve, passing the remaining sauce in a gravy boat.

1 (3-pound) boneless pork loin roast

1/4 cup all-purpose flour

1 (.7-ounce) packet dry Italian salad dressing mix

3 tablespoons olive oil (optional)

1 sprig fresh rosemary (optional)

4 sprigs fresh sage leaves (optional)

1/2 cup dry white wine

1 cup water

2 chicken bouillon cubes, crushed

1 (5-ounce) packet creamy mushroom sauce mix or 3 tablespoons instant potato flakes

Chopped fresh parsley leaves

Ham and Turkey Lasagna Alfredo

3 to 4 (10-ounce)
  containers refrigerated
  Alfredo sauce
9 to 12 lasagna noodles
1 (9-ounce) package
  shaved cured ham
1 (9-ounce) package
  shaved roasted turkey
  breast
2 to 3 cups shredded
  mozzarella cheese (8 to
  12 ounces)

This quick lasagna is an assembled dish of prepared ingredients yet it is elegant enough for a special lunch or dinner. Feel free to make as many layers of noodles filled with meat, sauce, and cheese as you wish.

1. Line a 6-quart slow cooker with aluminum foil in a crisscross pattern and gloss the foil with nonstick cooking spray.

2. Spread 1/2 cup of sauce over the bottom of the foil. Arrange 3 to 5 noodles over the sauce, breaking them to fit. Spread another 3/4 cup of sauce over the noodles and cover with the shredded cheese. Layer several overlapping slices of ham and turkey breast. Cover the meat with a thin layer of sauce and cheese. Continue alternating the ingredients and layers, ending with a top layer of cheese.

3. Cover, set the heat on low, and cook for 2 1/2 to 3 hours, until the cheese is melted, the sides are crusty and brown, and a knife inserts easily in the center. If necessary, this may be held on warm for up to 1 hour.

4. Remove the lasagna from the slow cooker by lifting up on the foil. Place the lasagna on a cutting board and allow it to sit for several minutes before cutting into wedges. Serve with any extra leftover Alfredo sauce, if desired.

Spiced Tomato BBQ Spare Ribs

Spare ribs naturally take on all sorts of flavors when they are cooked. Here is a riff on a southern barbecue sauce, created especially for the slow cooker. Have the butcher cut the slab of ribs into serving-size pieces of 2 to 4 ribs each.

4 to 5 pounds pork spare ribs, cut into serving-size pieces, trimmed of excess fat
1 cup ketchup
1 cup cola (not diet)
1 tablespoon dried minced onion
1 tablespoon paprika
1 tablespoon white vinegar
Dash of hot pepper flakes

1. Shape a piece of heavy-duty aluminum foil to fit a 6-quart slow cooker, leaving an overhang. Gloss the foil with nonstick cooking spray.

2. Arrange the ribs in the slow cooker, trying to expose as many meaty parts as possible.

3. In a measuring cup, whisk to combine the ketchup, cola, onion, paprika, vinegar, and pepper flakes. Pour the sauce over the ribs. Cover, set the heat on low, and cook for 5 to 6 hours, until the meat is tender but not falling off the bone (unless you like it that way). Turn off the heat, remove the cover, and allow the ribs to sit.

4. If time permits, lift up on the foil and place the ribs, foil, and liquid in the sink together. Preheat the broiler to high. Using tongs remove the ribs from the foil and arrange on a foil-lined broiler pan. Broil the ribs 2 to 4 inches from the heat for 5 to 10 minutes or until lightly scorched on top. If time is short, skip this step.

5. Place the ribs on a platter and serve immediately.

Barbecued Pork Loin

1 or 2 pork tenderloins
   (about 3 pounds total)
3/4 cup unsweetened apple
   or white grape juice
2 tablespoons sugar
2 tablespoons soy sauce
1 tablespoon white vinegar
1 teaspoon ground ginger
   or freshly grated ginger
   root
4 garlic cloves, minced
Pinch of pepper or to taste
7 1/2 teaspoons cornstarch
3 tablespoons cold water
Soft hamburger or soft
   sandwich rolls, to serve

The seasoning for this simple recipe has definite Asian flavors, but that can be changed to suit the occasion, such as adding balsamic vinegar and Italian spices. The results are similar to pulled pork barbecue and should be served on soft rolls.

1. Gloss the pot of a 5- to 6-quart slow cooker with nonstick cooking spray or use a plastic liner.

2. Score the fat on top of the pork with a small knife and place meat in the slow cooker.

3. In a small bowl, whisk together the juice, sugar, soy sauce, vinegar, ginger, garlic, and pepper. Pour over the pork loins. Cover, set the heat on low, and cook for 6 to 8 hours, or cook on high for 3 1/2 to 4 hours.

4. Remove the pork from the slow cooker and place on a cutting board. Allow it to sit for about 15 minutes.

5. Leave the slow cooker uncovered and set the heat on high. Whisk the cornstarch and water together in a measuring cup and stir into the sauce to thicken. Simmer several minutes while whisking occasionally until the desired consistency is reached (too brief a cooking time results in a bitter-tasting sauce).

6. Slice the meat and place on the buns with a little sauce.

Cuban Black Bean and Pork Stew

This recipe resembles one served at Calle Ocho (Eighth Street), a restaurant in Miami's Cuban district. The distinctive seasonings make for a brightly flavored sauce, which goes well over saffron rice.

1. Gloss the pot of a 5- to 6-quart slow cooker with nonstick cooking spray.

2. If time permits, preheat a large skillet until very hot. Add the oil and brown the meat on two sides. Transfer the meat to the cooker. Pour some of the beef broth into the skillet, scraping up any pieces sticking to the bottom. Add the water, tomatoes, wine, and vinegar, and heat until steaming. Pour the liquid over the meat in the cooker. If short on time, place the meat cubes in the slow cooker. Pour the broth, water, tomatoes, wine, and vinegar over the meat and mix.

3. Stir in the onion, bell pepper, chiles, raisins, garlic, cinnamon, cumin, coriander, oregano, and marjoram. Thinly slice 1 lime and float the slices on top of the food in the cooker.

4. Cover, set the heat on low, and cook for 6 to 7 hours. Stir in the black beans. Continue to cook another hour, until the meat is fork-tender.

5. Ladle the stew from the slow cooker into soup bowls. Cut the remaining lime into 8 sections and serve with each bowl of stew (a squeeze of lime juice brings out the flavors).

2 tablespoons olive oil

3 pounds boneless pork, cut into 1-inch chunks

1 (10 3/4-ounce) can condensed beef broth, plus 1 can water

1 (16-ounce) can stewed tomatoes

1 cup dry white wine

1/4 cup red wine vinegar

1 medium onion, thinly sliced

1 green bell pepper, cored, seeded, and quartered, sliced crosswise

1 (4.5-ounce) can green chiles

1/2 cup raisins

2 garlic cloves, finely chopped

1 teaspoon ground cinnamon

1 teaspoon ground cumin

1 teaspoon ground coriander

1/2 teaspoon dried oregano

1/2 teaspoon dried marjoram

2 limes

1 (14.5-ounce) can black beans, drained, rinsed

Poultry and Seafood

The most familiar poultry we eat—chicken and turkey—both provide low-fat protein and a range of B vitamins, and they can be economically, elegantly, and simply prepared, as the recipes in this chapter illustrate. Chicken, most especially, is like a blank canvas on which different cooking techniques and a range of spices and herbs result in colorful, flavor-packed feasting. The slow cooker also does a beautiful job cooking turkey breast, transforming it into a moist and scrumptious meal.

Loved by just about everyone as a source of vital omega-3 oils and other nutrients, fish and seafood have at last come into their own. This chapter uses simple preparations that transform easily available seafood choices into extraordinary one-dish meals, a treat for all.

Chicken Curry

Serves about 6

This is an exotically seasoned dish created from supermarket ingredients, and it's a cinch to put together. White rice is the perfect accompaniment to this fragrant preparation.

1. Gloss the pot of a 5- to 6-quart slow cooker with nonstick cooking spray or use a slow cooker liner.

2. Pat the chicken with damp paper towels. Trim off any excess skin and visible fat flaps.

3. If time permits, warm the oil in a large skillet over medium heat and brown the chicken. Place the chicken in the slow cooker as it is done browning, set the heat on low, and cover. In the same skillet, sauté the onions and garlic until soft. Stir in the ginger, curry powder, paprika, turmeric, cumin, and pepper. Stir in the tomatoes and continue cooking until hot. Slowly pour the sauce over the chicken. If time is short, remove the skin and place the chicken directly into the pot. Mix onions, garlic, seasonings, and tomatoes in another bowl. Pour this mixture over the chicken.

4. Cover and cook on low for 6 to 7 hours or until the chicken is fork-tender. Remove chicken and place on a large platter.

5. Spoon the sauce over the chicken and serve.

3 pounds assorted chicken parts (drumsticks, thighs, breasts)
1/4 cup olive oil (optional)
2 medium onions, chopped
2 teaspoons minced garlic
1 1/2 teaspoons ground ginger
2 teaspoons mild curry powder
1 teaspoon paprika
Pinch of turmeric
Pinch of ground cumin
Pinch of black pepper
1 (14.5-ounce) can diced tomatoes

Turkey Breast and Vegetables

1 chicken bouillon cube
1/4 cup hot water
3 medium carrots, peeled, trimmed, cut into lengthwise quarters
3 medium celery ribs, cut in half
4 medium Yukon Gold potatoes, halved
1 small onion, sliced
1 whole frozen turkey breast with skin, thawed
2 tablespoons unsalted butter, melted
2 tablespoons finely chopped fresh parsley
1 tablespoon dried thyme
1 teaspoon paprika
1/2 teaspoon salt
1/4 teaspoon black pepper

Turkey breast and the slow cooker make a perfect marriage. Moisture dripping on to the breast tenderizes and enhances the beautiful natural qualities of this lean meat, which in other cooking conditions might emerge dry and stringy. Assorted vegetables season the turkey and make a side dish for the meal.

1. Dissolve the bouillon cube in the hot water; set aside.

2. Gloss the pot of a 5- to 6-quart slow cooker with nonstick cooking spray or use a slow cooker liner.

3. Place the carrots, celery, potatoes, and onion on the bottom of the pot. Pat the turkey breast with damp paper towels. Place the turkey breast in the pot skin side up. Brush with melted butter and sprinkle with the parsley, thyme, paprika, salt, and pepper.

4. Add the chicken broth to the pot. Cover, set the heat on low, and cook for 6 to 8 hours, until the vegetables and turkey are fork-tender.

5. Remove the turkey from the pot when done and place on a cutting board. Allow the turkey to sit for 15 minutes before slicing. Place overlapping slices on a serving dish and serve with the vegetables.

Chicken Piccata

It's as easy and tasty as a chicken dish gets. With wine, lemon juice, and the trinity of herbs—sage, basil, and rosemary—for flavor and attractiveness, this is an herb-seasoned variation on the classic preparation.

1. Gloss the pot of a 5- to 6-quart slow cooker with nonstick cooking spray.

2. Pat the chicken with damp paper towels. Combine the flour, salt, pepper, sage, basil, and rosemary in a small bowl. Rub into the skin of the chicken. Thinly slice 1 lemon and set aside.

3. Warm the olive oil in a large skillet over medium heat and brown the chicken on both sides, beginning with the skin side (this can be done the night before to save time as well). Place the chicken in the slow cooker as the pieces are done and put a lemon slice on each piece. (There will be more than one layer of chicken, so stagger the pieces.) Pour the wine into the skillet, scraping up any pieces sticking to the bottom, and then slowly pour the hot wine over the chicken. Combine the butter and vegetable oil and pour over the chicken.

4. Cover, set the heat on low, and cook for 6 to 7 hours, or cook on high for 4 to 5 hours, until the chicken is fork-tender. Cut the other lemon into wedges and serve the chicken with the wedges.

2 to 3 pounds assorted chicken parts (drumsticks, thighs, breasts)
1/3 cup all-purpose flour
1 teaspoon salt
1/2 teaspoon black pepper
2 teaspoons dried sage
2 teaspoons dried basil
2 teaspoons dried rosemary
2 lemons
3 tablespoons olive oil
1/2 cup white wine
2 tablespoons butter, melted
2 tablespoons vegetable oil

Apricot-Caper Chicken with Kalamata Olives

3 pounds assorted chicken parts (drumsticks, thighs, breasts)
1/2 cup dried apricots, quartered
1/2 cup Kalamata olives or other pitted black olives
2 garlic cloves, finely chopped
1 tablespoon dried basil
2 tablespoons drained capers, rinsed
1/2 cup orange juice
1/4 cup white wine vinegar
Freshly ground black pepper to taste
1 medium naval orange

This recipe uses ingredients favored by the Turks and Greeks. Basil and capers are found in Turkish cuisine while apricots and Kalamata olives are well known Greek favorites. Serve this dish over white rice or orzo, the rice-shaped pasta.

1. Gloss the pot of a 5- to 6-quart slow cooker with nonstick cooking spray.

2. Pat the chicken with damp paper towels. Remove any visible fat and place them in the slow cooker.

3. Top with the apricots, olives, garlic, basil, and capers. Add the orange juice and vinegar. Season with pepper as desired.

4. Grate the zest (orange-colored rind) from the orange and add to the cooker. Slice the orange and lay the slices over the top of the food. Cover, set the heat on low, and cook for 6 to 7 hours, until the chicken is fork-tender. (Do not to overcook the chicken as the meat will fall off the bones and lack attractiveness.)

Sicilian Tomato Sauce with Salmon

Tomato sauce prepared using butter and oil is a practice typical of cooks from southern Italy. This versatile sauce serves well whether over pasta or with polenta.

1. Place the butter, oil, garlic, tomato sauce, tomatoes, Italian seasoning, olives, salt, pepper, and crushed red pepper in a 4- to 5-quart slow cooker. Stir to combine the ingredients. Cover, set the heat on low, and cook for 5 to 6 hours, or cook on high for 4 hours.

2. Turn the tail and thinner sections of the salmon under so the fillet is uniform in thickness; place it in the sauce, spooning some over the top, and cook another 30 minutes on low.

3. Transfer the fish to a heated platter. Spoon the sauce over the fish. Sprinkle parsley over the fish and serve immediately with pasta, dividing the salmon among the plates.

2 tablespoons unsalted butter, melted
4 tablespoons olive oil
1 tablespoon finely minced garlic
1 (29-ounce) can tomato sauce
1 (28-ounce) can diced tomatoes
1 tablespoon dried Italian seasoning
1/2 cup pitted Kalamata olives, rinsed
1/2 teaspoon salt
1/4 teaspoon black pepper
1/4 teaspoon crushed red pepper
1 pound salmon fillets, without skin, rinsed, patted dry
1/4 cup chopped fresh parsley
Cooked pasta, to serve

Seafood Stew

2 medium baking potatoes, peeled, cut into 1/4-inch slices
1 large yellow onion, coarsely chopped
4 tablespoons olive oil
1 (16-ounce) can diced tomatoes, drained, reserving the liquid
1 (15-ounce) can tomato sauce
2 to 3 teaspoons minced garlic
2 to 3 teaspoons dried thyme
1/4 teaspoon crushed red pepper
1 teaspoon paprika
1/2 teaspoon salt
1/2 teaspoon black pepper
2 (15-ounce) cans chopped clams, drained, reserving the liquor

2 bay leaves
3/4 pound skinless, boneless cod fillets, cut into 2-inch pieces
6 sea scallops

6 large uncooked shrimp, shelled
1/4 cup chopped fresh parsley
Garlic toast, to serve

Although this stew has a long list of ingredients and involves two steps, it is an exceptional dish filled with tasty vegetables and wholesome fish and seafood. Ladle the ingredients over garlic toast placed in the bottom of individual soup bowls.

1. Gloss the pot of a 5- to 6-quart slow cooker with nonstick cooking spray.

2. Place the potatoes and onion in the bottom of the pot. Toss with the oil, tomatoes, tomato sauce, garlic, thyme, crushed red pepper, paprika, salt, and pepper. Add the tomato liquid, clam liquor, bay leaves, and enough water to equal 3 cups. Cover, set the heat on low, and cook 6 to 7 hours, until the potatoes are tender.

3. Rinse the cod fillets and scallops in cold water and pat dry with paper towels. Turn the heat to high, add the cod, scallops, shrimp, and reserved clams and cook 30 to 45 minutes. Stir in the chopped parsley.

4. Remove and discard bay leaves. Place a garlic toast in the bottom of each soup bowl. Ladle the soup from the slow cooker into the bowls and serve.

Chicken in Beer Sauce

This tasty meal from Belgium is a substantial winter dish that is deliciously made with either a lager beer or dark ale. It is as fine a family meal as it is a company or potluck dish.

1. Gloss the pot of a 5- to 6-quart slow cooker with nonstick cooking spray or use a slow cooker liner.

2. Pat the chicken with damp paper towels. Trim off any excess skin and fat flaps. Place the onions, carrots, potatoes, and bacon in the bottom of the pot. Drizzle with 2 tablespoons of the oil and toss to coat. Combine the flour with the salt and pepper on a sheet of wax paper. Roll the chicken pieces in the flour.

3. Warm the remaining 4 tablespoons of oil in a large skillet over medium heat and brown the chicken on both sides, beginning with the skin side. Place the chicken in the slow cooker over the vegetables as the pieces are done. (There will be more than one layer of chicken; so stagger the arrangement.) Pour the beer and vinegar into the skillet, scraping up any pieces stuck to the bottom. Gradually pour the beer mixture over the chicken.

4. Cover, set the heat on low, and cook for 6 to 7 hours, or cook on high for 4 to 5 hours, until the chicken is fork-tender. Sprinkle with the chopped parsley and serve with hot buttered noodles.

2 1/2 to 3 pounds assorted chicken parts (drumsticks, thighs, breasts)
1 1/2 to 2 pounds (about 6 medium) yellow onions, cut into quarters
1 pound baby carrots, rinsed
2 medium Yukon Gold potatoes, cut into quarters
1/2 pound sliced bacon, cooked until crisp
6 tablespoons olive oil
1/4 cup all-purpose flour
Salt and pepper to taste
1 (12-ounce) bottle or can of lager beer or ale
2 tablespoons white wine or cider vinegar
Chopped fresh parsley, to serve
Hot buttered noodles, to serve

Desserts

As the final course of any meal, desserts such as these five make a sweet conclusion. Everyone enjoys homespun desserts, made with style and the slow cooker excels in this category. Whether you have a sweet tooth craving, rich, dark chocolate, or favor the wholesome goodness of classic fruit, or just can't get enough creamy cheesecake, these sweet delights will be tempting, even after a satisfying meal.

Apple Cobbler
Studded with Cherries

This enjoyable dessert really looks like its name—an old-time cobbler with a light bumpy topping. So versatile, this combination of ingredients lends homey warmth to potluck brunches as well as to casual dinners and family meals. The dried cherries lend a tart contrast to the sweet apple filling.

1 (21-ounce) can apple pie filling
3/4 teaspoon cinnamon
1/3 cup dried cherries
1 cup all-purpose flour
1/3 cup sugar
1 teaspoon baking powder
1/4 teaspoon salt
3/4 cup milk
1 teaspoon vanilla extract
2 tablespoons unsalted butter, melted

1. Gloss a 3 1/2- to 4-quart slow cooker with nonstick cooking spray.

2. Place the pie filling in the cooker and stir in the cinnamon and dried cherries.

3. Combine the flour, sugar, baking powder, and salt in a medium bowl. Stir in the milk, vanilla, and butter. Spoon the dough over the apple mixture.

4. Cover, set the heat on high, and cook for 2 to 2 1/2 hours, until a tester inserted into the center comes out clean. Turn the slow cooker off and remove the cover. Allow the dessert to sit for 20 minutes before spooning into dessert dishes.

Chocolate Spoon Cake

Topping:

**1/3 cup unsweetened cocoa
powder, sifted if lumpy**

1/3 cup sugar

**1/3 cup tightly packed
brown sugar**

Cake:

1 cup all-purpose flour

**1/3 cup unsweetened cocoa
powder, sifted if lumpy**

1/2 cup sugar

**1 1/2 teaspoons baking
powder**

1/4 teaspoon salt

1 cup milk

**5 tablespoons unsalted
butter, melted**

1 1/2 cups boiling water

*This rich but feather-light cake makes its own sauce on the bottom
while cooking. Use a large serving spoon to dig down deep and
scoop up that intensely flavored dark chocolate sauce.*

1. Gloss a 3 1/2- to 4-quart slow cooker with nonstick cooking spray.

2. Whisk the cocoa, sugar, and brown sugar for the topping in a medium bowl. Transfer
to a sheet of wax paper. Set aside.

3. Put the flour, cocoa, sugar, and baking powder for the cake in the topping bowl.
Make a well in the center and add the milk and butter, whisking the mixture until well
combined and smooth. Transfer the mixture to the cooker and spread evenly using a
spatula.

4. Sprinkle the topping mixture over the cake. Pour the boiling water slowly and evenly
over the topping without stirring. Cover, set the heat on high, and cook for 2 to 2 1/2
hours, until the center is almost set. Uncover and allow the mixture to sit for about 15
minutes before serving into dessert dishes.

Creamy Rice Pudding

Serves about 6

This slow cooker rice pudding tastes as good as many of the other stirred rice puddings, but this is made without any stirring and also is free of any top skin. Cardamom adds an interesting flavor to the pudding, but it doesn't suffer if the spice is unavailable.

1. Gloss a 2-quart soufflé dish with baking spray. Place a trivet or flat roasting rack or a wreath fashioned from aluminum foil in a 6-quart round slow cooker. Place the soufflé dish on the trivet. Pour about 2 cups of hot water into the slow cooker around the soufflé dish. Cover and turn the heat to high.

2. If time permits and you are using the cardamom pods, peel and remove the seeds using a paring knife, and warm them in a dry skillet for a few minutes over medium heat until aromatic. Pour the seeds onto foil, double it over and lightly pound with a mallet or spoon to make particles.

3. Mix the roasted cardamom, if using, with the rice, milk, sugar, eggs, and zest in a large glass measuring cup. Pour the mixture into the soufflé dish. Bury the cinnamon sticks in the rice pudding. Cover the soufflé dish tightly with aluminum foil. Cover the slow cooker and cook on high for 2 hours. At the end of this time, the rice pudding should be thick and creamy.

4. Turn the slow cooker off, uncover the slow cooker, and allow the pudding to cool for about 15 minutes. Remove the soufflé dish using pot holders and place on a towel. Remove the foil, take out the cinnamon sticks, and stir in the vanilla. Smooth the surface. Sprinkle with cinnamon, cover, and refrigerate. Enjoy warm, cool, or cold—whichever temperature you prefer.

3 cardamom pods (optional)
2 cups cooked basmati rice
3 1/3 cups milk
2/3 cup sugar
2 large eggs, beaten
Zest of 1 orange
2 cinnamon sticks
1 teaspoon vanilla extract
Ground cinnamon, to garnish

Creamy Cheesecake

Crust:
**1/2 cup graham cracker
    crumbs**
2 tablespoons sugar
**3 tablespoons unsalted
    butter, melted**

Cake:
**2 (8-ounce) packages cream
    cheese, cut into thirds,
    softened**
2 large eggs, lightly beaten
Zest of 1 lemon
Zest of 1 orange
1 teaspoon vanilla extract
**1 (14-ounce) can sweetened
    condensed milk**
**1/4 cup sour cream (not
    nonfat)**

This pleasantly sweet version of cheesecake holds its own among the best for creamy texture, attractiveness, and ease of preparation. The top remains intact and does not split, as a cheesecake often does when baked in the oven.

1. Place a trivet or flat roasting rack or a wreath fashioned from aluminum foil in the bottom of a 5- to 6-quart round slow cooker. Gloss an 8-inch springform pan with nonstick cooking spray.

2. Prepare the crust by combining the graham cracker crumbs, sugar, and butter in a small bowl. Reserve 2 tablespoonfuls of the mixture and press the rest into the bottom of the springform pan. Set the pan in the slow cooker, making certain it is stable and level.

3. For the filling, combine the cream cheese, eggs, zests, vanilla, milk, and sour cream in a food processor by pulsing on/off several times. Scrape the mixture from around the sides and up from the bottom a couple of times. Pulse on/off 10 to 15 times to mix the batter until smooth. (A few small lumps bake to smoothness, but the larger ones do not.) Scrape again. Pulse several times again until the mixture is smooth.

4. Pour the cream cheese mixture to the springform pan over the crust. Sprinkle the reserved crust mixture on the top. Cover, set the heat on high, and cook for 2 1/2 to 3 hours, until the center is almost set. (Allow the cake to absorb any moisture on the top of the cake.)

5. Turn off the heat and allow the cake to sit in the slow cooker for 1 to 2 hours. Uncover, remove the pan from the slow cooker, and allow it to cool completely on a cake rack before covering and refrigerating overnight.

6. Slide a knife around the sides of the pan and cheesecake. Gently remove the sides before slicing.

Raisin and Date-Stuffed Baked Apples

5 to 6 medium baking
   apples, washed, cored
5 to 6 large pitted dates
1 cup dark raisins
1 cup water
1/2 to 3/4 cup tightly
   packed light brown
   sugar
4 to 5 tablespoons
   unsalted butter
4 tablespoons light or dark
   corn syrup
1 to 1 1/2 teaspoons
   cinnamon

Slow-cooked apples make a wonderful dessert and breakfast treat. The raisins and dates are full of sweetness, so adjust the sugar to suit your family's taste. Use dried cranberries, cherries, or chopped dried apricots as stuffing alternatives.

1. Gloss the pot of a 4- to 6-quart slow cooker with nonstick cooking spray.

2. Remove a wide strip of peel down 1/4 from the top of each apple. Slice off some of the bottom to make it sit level. Stuff a date into each cavity and fill with raisins. Arrange the apples in the slow cooker and set the heat on high.

3. Bring the water, brown sugar, butter, corn syrup, and cinnamon to a boil in a small saucepan. Stir 3 to 4 minutes at a gentle boil to dissolve the sugar. Cool for 1 to 2 minutes, then spoon the hot syrup over the apples. Cover, set the heat on low, and cook for 2 to 4 hours, until the apples are fork-tender.

4. Spoon the sauce over the apples and serve.

Notes

Notes

Notes

Notes

Notes

Notes

Notes

Notes

Notes

Acknowledgements

To Jim, my HONEY, you gave me the room and patience to make my mess—to create and test, write recipes, and to have a family of five slow cookers burbling away on the counter. Who would believe you sometimes ate two meals a day of my trial runs?

Thanks to all of my family, colleagues and relatives for answering my call for *51 Fast & Fun Slow Cooker Recipes:* **Jeff and Anna Kostelni, Natalie Kostelni, Maria Kostelni, Hugo and Judy Kostelni, Dalia Binnie, Barbara Dod Whittle, Karen Vartran, Barbara Lauterbach, Luanne Traud, and CiCi Williamson.**

To Lindsay Brown, skillful editor, your knowledge of food and grammar is extraordinary. To Richard Perry, CEO of Collectors Press, many thanks for extending me the pleasure of having a good time while writing another cookbook for your creative publishing house.